Happy Birthday
Jenny, x
Love & hugs,
Sue & Roger xxx

Flowerpot Farm

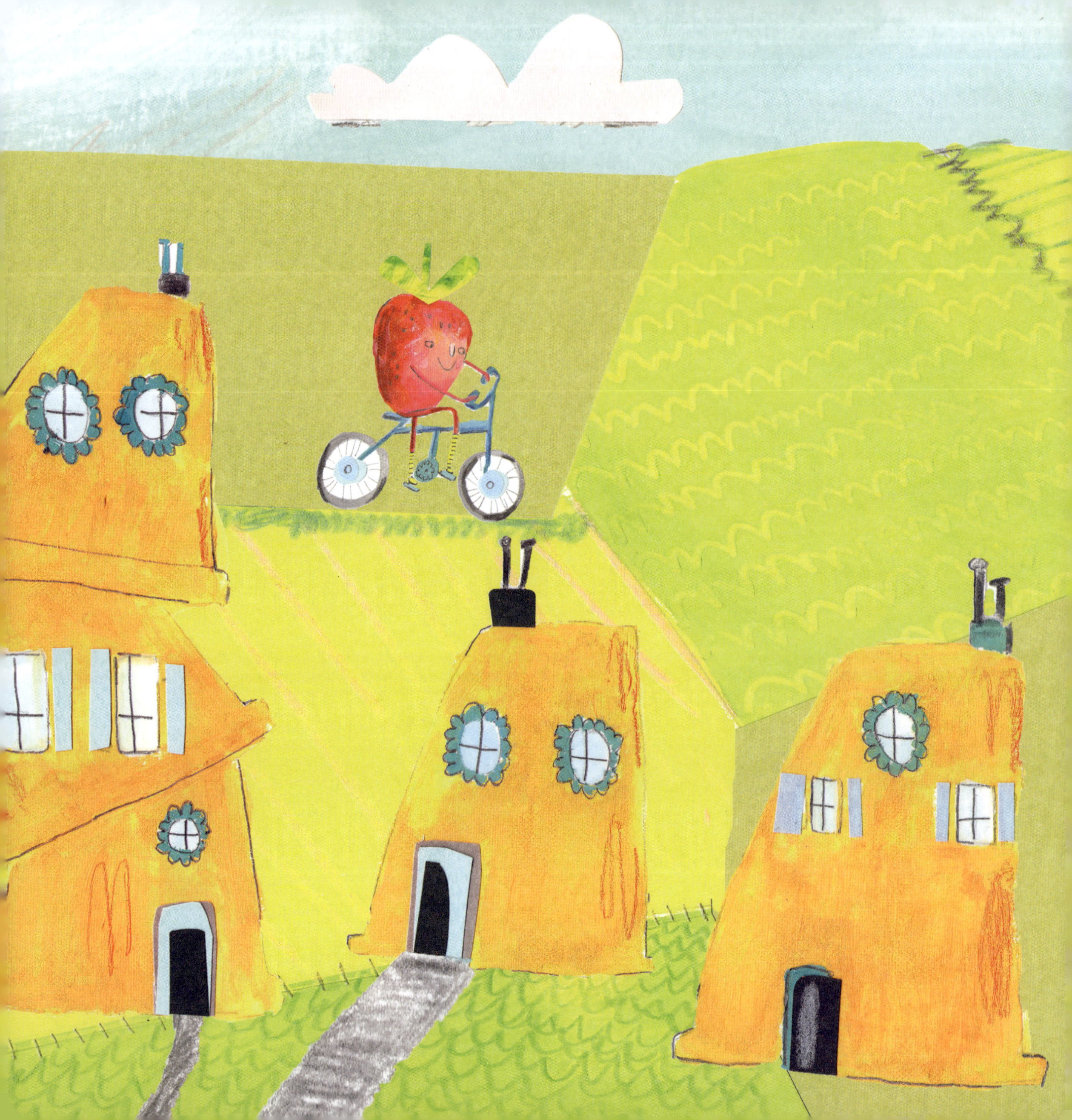

Flowerpot Farm

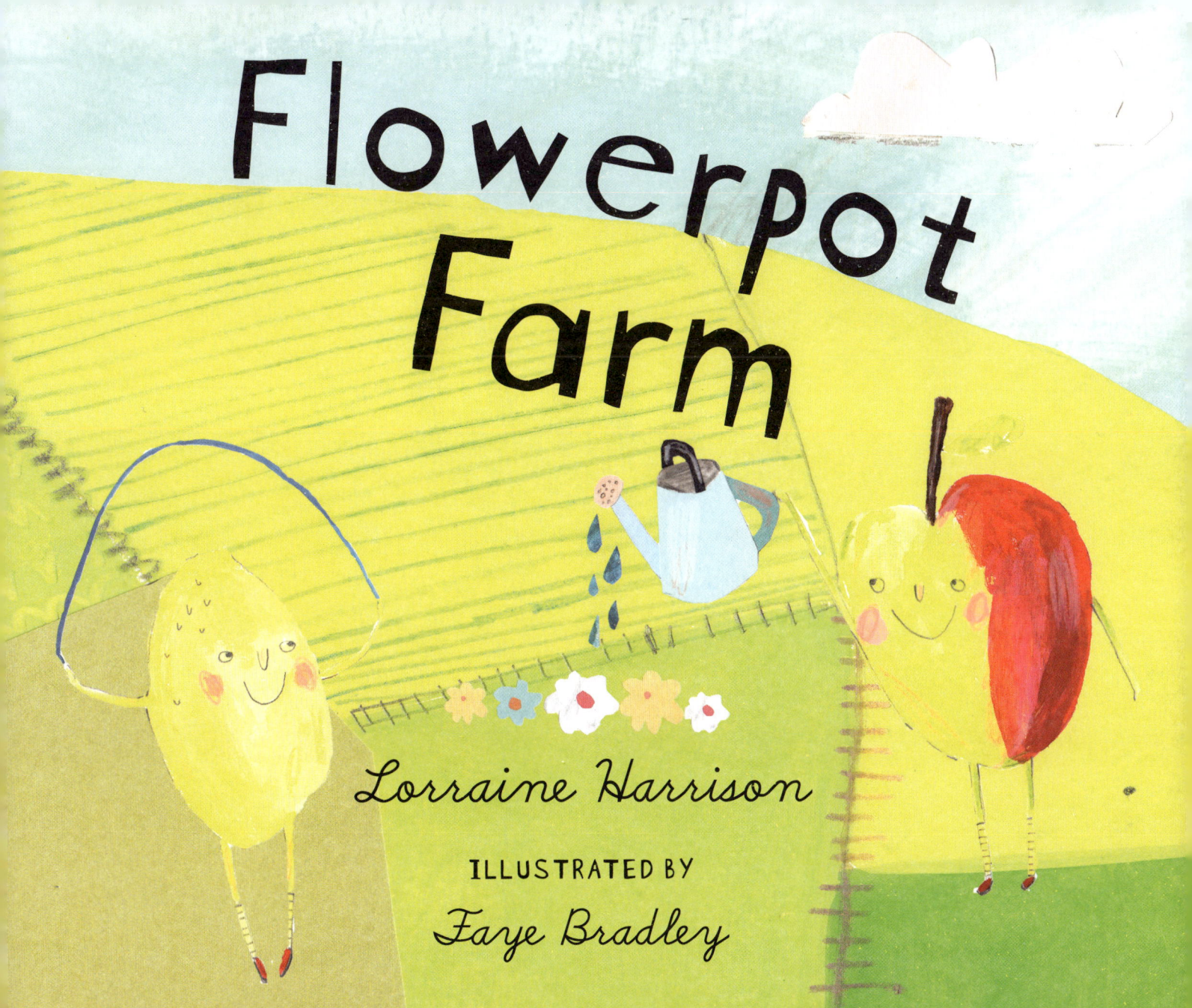

Lorraine Harrison

ILLUSTRATED BY
Faye Bradley

Ivy Kids

First published in the UK in 2014 by

Ivy Press

210 High Street
Lewes
East Sussex BN7 2NS
United Kingdom
www.ivypress.co.uk

Copyright 2013 by Ivy Press
All rights reserved. No part of this book may be reproduced or transmitted in any form or by any means, electronic or mechanical, including photocopying, recording, or by any information storage-and-retrieval system, without written permission from the copyright holder.

ISBN: 978-1-78240-081-3

This book was conceived, designed & produced by

Ivy Press

CREATIVE DIRECTOR	Peter Bridgewater
MANAGING EDITOR	Hazel Songhurst
COMMISSIONING EDITOR	Georgia Amson-Bradshaw
PROJECT EDITOR	Susie Behar
ART DIRECTOR	Kim Hankinson
DESIGNERS	Fiona Grant and Kevin Knight

Printed in China

Colour origination by Ivy Press Reprographics

10 9 8 7 6 5 4 3 2 1

Contents

- 6 Hello from Flowerpot Farm
- 8 Getting Started on Flowerpot Farm
- 10 Sowing Seeds
- 12 Growing Seeds
- 14 Lovely Labels
- 16 Floral Magic
- 28 Vroom Vroom Veg
- 40 Fabulous Fruit
- 50 Flowerpot Farm Friends
- 52 Meet the Pollinators
- 54 Meet the Garden Guests
- 56 Wriggling Worms
- 58 Meet the Garden Pests
- 60 Winter on the Farm
- 62 Index
- 64 Goodbye from Flowerpot Farm

FAB FRUITS!

Hello from Flowerpot Farm

Would you like to be a farmer on your very own Flowerpot Farm? Then put your boots on, grab a trowel and get busy!

You can grow scrummy strawberries, juicy courgettes and sun-loving sunflowers. You can plant a little apple tree or blueberry bush and watch it grow and then eat the tasty fruit.

You can watch as butterflies and bees buzz about your flowerpots looking for nectar. Why not make your very own house for those wiggly worms that are so helpful in the garden and some fun food for hungry birds in winter?

And when you've harvested your bumper crop of fruit and vegetables, an adult can help you turn them into tasty treats for your tummy. Yum!

So, green fingers at the ready – it's time to get farming!

Getting Started on Flowerpot Farm

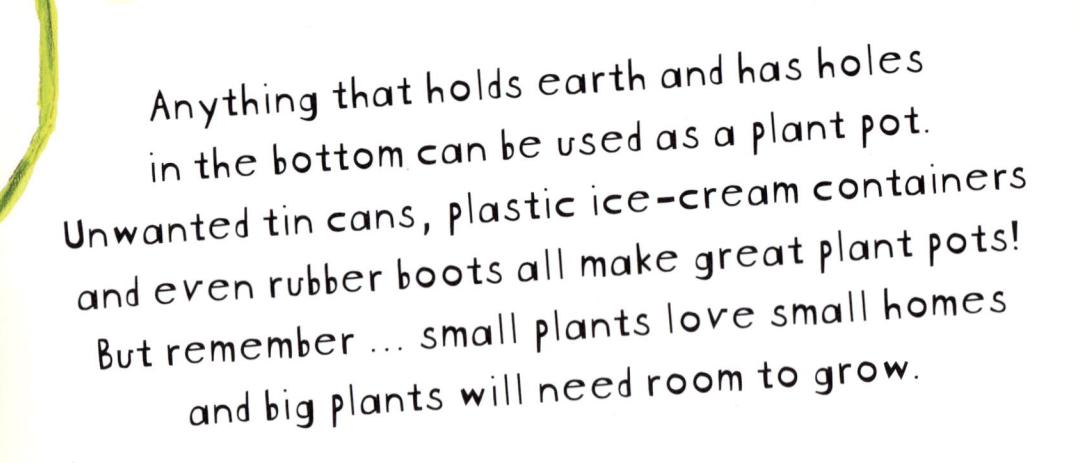

Anything that holds earth and has holes in the bottom can be used as a plant pot. Unwanted tin cans, plastic ice-cream containers and even rubber boots all make great plant pots! But remember ... small plants love small homes and big plants will need room to grow.

Ask a grown-up to put some holes in the bottom of your container so that water can drain away – plants don't like to have wet feet!

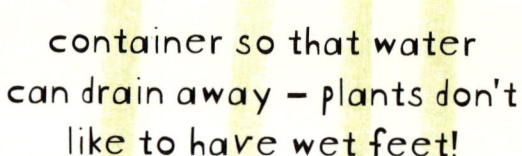

To keep your plants happy, grow them in a special soil called compost. And, just like people, plants need to eat. Buy a bottle of liquid feed and add a few drops to your plant water once a week. Your plants will grow big and strong.

And of course you'll need seeds! If you know a grown-up gardener, they might be able to give you some. Or, you can buy some at a shop.

Tools at the ready!

A watering can for watering.

A little shovel, called a trowel, for moving compost.

A garden fork for weeding.

Sowing seeds

Many plants begin life as little seeds. Planting your seeds is called 'sowing'. Watch as the tiny little seeds turn into plants and grow bigger and bigger. Magic!

Things you need

- Seeds
- Tray
- Compost
- Watering can
- Label

step 1

Find a tray. An old ice-cream tub is perfect! Ask a grown-up to put some small holes in the bottom so the water can run away.

Fill the tray with compost but leave a space between the compost and the top of the tray.

step 2

Press each seed very gently into the compost. Don't press in the seed too deeply, and leave space between each one.

step 3

Water the compost. Place a label in the tray with the name of the plant on it.

lettuce

step 4

Put the tray on a sunny windowsill. Visit it every day and if the compost feels dry add a little water. In a few days some seeds turn into little plants, called seedlings.

Other types of seeds may take a few weeks. So be patient!

Growing seeds

Your little seedlings need lots of care to help them grow into strong and healthy plants. They also need space for their roots to spread out as they get bigger.

true leaves

first leaves

stem

roots

Things you need

- Small plant pots • Compost • Broken bits of pot
- Watering can • Labels • An old pencil

step 1

When bigger leaves begin to grow out of the first two little leaves, the seedlings need more space to grow. These bigger leaves are called 'true leaves'.

growing tip

Lunchtime is usually the hottest time of day. If you water the seedlings in the morning or in the evening they will stay wet for longer.

step 2

Put broken bits of pot into the bottom of a small flowerpot. Fill with compost. Press your thumb into the compost to make a little hole.

step 3

Using your thumb and finger gently take hold of the top leaves. Use an old pencil to carefully lift the seedling's roots out of the compost.

step 4

Put the roots into the hole in the compost. Gently press the compost over the roots. Don't touch the roots or the stem as this hurts the young plant.

step 5

Label your flowerpots so you know which plant is which! Water a little every day and watch the plants grow.

Lovely labels

It is important to label your plants so you know which plant is in which pot. You can make your own plant labels from pieces of card and lolly sticks.

step 1

Ask an adult to help you cut out a star, circle or flower shape, about 3cm (1in) wide.

Things you need

- Lolly sticks
- Card • Paint
- Paintbrush • Glue
- Scissors
- Clear outdoor varnish

step 2

Paint it in on one side to make it pretty.

step 3

Glue the shape to the top of the lolly stick.

step 4

Write the plant name on the stick. Paint it with clear outdoor varnish. Put your pots together in a big group. This looks lovely and makes watering them easier.

Pretty up your pots

Paint can be messy, so make sure an adult helps you! Wash your plant pots and let them dry. Paint them, using outdoor paint if you have it. You could paint a happy face or the moon and stars or butterflies, bees and birds. Or you could paint patterns like spots and stripes. When the pots are dry, paint with outdoor varnish to protect them.

Floral Magic

Fill your farm with flowerpots full of lovely flowers and you'll see butterflies and bees. They love visiting flowers with brightly coloured petals and sweet-smelling scents. Watch them flit from flower to flower.

When your flowers are looking beautiful, pick some and bring them indoors to put in a vase. To make a special present, tie them in a bunch and wrap in pretty paper.

Flower power

Do you know that flowers last longer if you pick them early in the morning before the sun is too hot? Remember to put them in water straight away.

Magic marigolds

These lovely yellow and golden flowers look like the sun! They grow from spring to summer and like to be hot so put them in the sunniest place on the farm.

Things you need

- Seeds • Pot • Broken bits of pot
- Compost • Plant food • Watering can • Labels

Plant in the spring!

step 1

Early in spring put some broken bits of pot into a big pot. Fill it with compost but not to the top.

step 2

Spread the seeds very thinly over the compost. Sprinkle a little more compost on top. Add a label and then water.

step 3

Put the pot in a warm, sunny place. You don't need to move the little seedlings into bigger pots. They will grow well where they are.

growing tip

Grow French marigolds next to tomatoes. Their strong smell keeps naughty pests like blackfly and whitefly away.

Tummy treats

You can eat the flowers of pot marigolds. The 'pot' in their name is a cooking pot, not a flowerpot! Add to salads or make yellow-coloured rice by adding a few petals to the cooking water.

step 4

Water your marigolds often. When you first see the pretty flowers you need to feed them once a week.

Super sweet peas

Sweet peas grow from spring to the end of summer. The flowers smell lovely! If you cut off the flowers when they have faded, more will grow. Cool!

Things you need

- Seeds • cardboard tubes
- Compost • Large pot
- Broken bits of pot
- Plant food • Watering can
- Labels • Bamboo canes or sticks • String

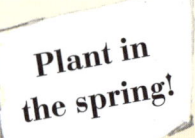

Plant in the spring!

TAKE CARE! Sweet-pea pods look a bit like peas but are very poisonous. NEVER eat them!

step 1
In spring fill the tubes with compost. Stand them upright in a tray. Sweet peas have long roots and like long pots.

step 2
Press one seed into each tube and cover with compost. Leave in a cool place indoors. Water your seeds a little bit, every other day.

step 3

When the plants are 10cm (4in) tall, pinch out the top two leaves. This makes the plants bushy.

step 4

When it gets warm take the plants outside. Put broken bits of pot in the large pot. Fill it with compost. Dig deep holes around the edge of the pot and put the tubes in the holes. Water every day and feed once a week.

step 5

Make a wigwam in the pot using the canes. As the plants grow taller, tie them to the wigwam.

Nice nasturtiums

Plants come in all different shapes and sizes. Some grow tall and thin. Some are bushy and others, like nasturtiums, like to trail around and climb up things.

Things you need

- Seeds • Pot • Broken bits of pot
- Compost • Plant food
- Watering can • Label

Plant in the spring!

step 1

In spring put broken bits of pot into a pot. Fill it with compost but not to the top. Make holes in the compost with your finger. Pop in the seeds and cover with more compost.

step 2

Add a label, water and put in a warm and sunny place. Watch and wait for the first leaves to appear.

step 3

Water your seedlings often. Then, when you see the first flowers, add some plant food to the water once a week.

growing tip

Stand a big pot upside down. Put your pot full of nasturtiums on top. See how the leaves and flowers trail and tumble to the ground.

Tummy treats

Add nasturtium flowers to salads to make them extra pretty. The leaves taste quite hot and peppery, a bit like watercress. Try them in your sandwiches!

Cheerful chives

Chives are herbs with purple pom-pom flowers. Their thin leaves are long green tubes and taste like onions. Cut the leaves with little scissors and add to salads.

Things you need

- Seeds • Pot
- Broken bits of pot
- Compost • Plant food
- Watering can • Label

Step 1

Early in spring put broken bits of pot into a pot. Fill with compost but not to the top. Spread the seeds thinly over the compost. Sprinkle a little more compost on top. Water and label.

Plant in the spring!

step 2

Chives do not like to be thirsty, so water your seeds often. Once they start to flower add liquid feed to the water once a week.

growing tip

Bring your pot of chives indoors in autumn. Put it on the kitchen windowsill and snip away all winter long.

Tummy treats

Jacket potatoes taste yummy with chive butter. Snip some chive leaves into little pieces. Mash some butter in a bowl until soft. Add the chives and mix with the butter. Pat into little balls and keep in the fridge until the potatoes are ready to eat.

Sunny sunflowers

Sunflowers grow from mid spring until autumn. They can grow very, very tall. Why don't you have a competition with your friends to see who can grow the tallest sunflower?

Things you need

- Seeds • Large pot
- Broken bits of pot • Compost
- Plant food • Watering can
- Label • Bamboo cane or stick
- String

Plant in the spring!

step 1

In spring put some broken bits of pot into a large pot. Fill with compost. Make three little holes in the centre with your finger. Press a seed in each hole and cover with compost.

step 2

Add a label and water a little every day. Place in a sunny spot.

step 3

If all three seeds turn into seedlings, wait and see which one grows best. Leave this one in the pot and gently pull out the others. Now watch this strong little plant grow and grow!

step 4

Water your sunflower every day. Once a week add some liquid feed to the water.

step 5

Put a bamboo cane or stick into the pot alongside the sunflower plant. Tie the stalk to the stick with string. This will stop it falling over as it grows taller.

Collecting seeds

In autumn sunflower heads turn downwards and look sad. By now the flower is full of seeds. When the seeds look dry ask a grown-up to cut off the flower head. Place it on a bird table and wait for birds to come and eat the seeds.

Vroom vroom veg

Imagine a plate full of tasty tomatoes, perfect potatoes and lovely lettuce all grown by you! It's easy for the flowerpot farmer — all you need are flowerpots, compost, seeds, water and sunshine.

Your farm friends

Did you know that some of the creatures that visit Flowerpot Farm can help you grow bigger and better vegetables?

home

Bees, butterflies, hoverflies and worms are all your helpmates down on the farm.

Perfect potatoes

Plant your salad potatoes in the spring and dig them up to eat in summer.

Things you need

- Seed salad potatoes • Big pot
- Broken bits of pot • Compost
- Plant food • Watering can • Label

Plant in the spring!

step 1
At the end of winter put the seed potatoes on a tray or egg box in a dry and light place indoors. Watch as little shoots called 'chits' appear.

TAKE CARE!
Never, ever eat potatoes that have turned green as they will give you a very bad tummy ache. Yuk!

step 2

When the weather starts to get warm put some broken bits of pot into a big pot. Fill half of the pot with compost.

growing tip

When the flowers appear, add feed to the water once a week. When the leaves die back, your crop is ready to pick!

step 3

Leave two chits on each potato but rub off the rest. Place the potatoes close together on the compost. Add more compost to cover them and water regularly.

step 4

When leaves appear add a bit more compost. Keep doing this until it almost reaches the top.

Long-lasting lettuces

If you sow 'cut-and-come-again' lettuce seeds, when you cut the leaves, they will grow back again! Sow a new pot of lettuces every two weeks and you'll have lettuces all summer long. Wow!

Things you need

- Seeds
- Pot
- Broken bits of pot
- Compost
- Plant food
- Watering can
- Label

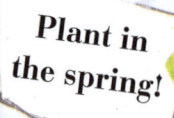

Plant in the spring!

step 1

In spring put broken bits of pot into a pot. Fill with compost. Spread the seeds very thinly over the compost. Sprinkle on a little more compost.

step 2

Add a label to your plant pot and water.

growing tip

Water your lettuces every morning. They don't like to sit in wet compost overnight!

step 3

Choose a cool place with a little shade for your lettuces.

step 4

When the plants are 10-15cm (4-6in) tall, cut the tops off with little scissors. Leave about 5cm (2in) of leaf. This will grow again. Magic!

Tummy treats

To make a scrummy salad, wash mixed salad leaves in water. Shake in a colander to dry. Tear into small pieces and put in a big bowl. Chop vegetables like tomatoes, cucumber and radishes into small chunks and add them. Sprinkle with olive oil, lemon juice, salt and pepper.

Red radishes and little onions

Radishes are one of the quickest crops to grow. They take only a few weeks! Spring onions are miniature onions with tall, thin leaves. Radishes and onions taste great in salads.

Things you need

- Seeds
- Pots
- Broken bits of pot
- Compost
- Watering can
- Label

step 1

Early in spring put broken pots in the bottom of a pot.

Fill with compost. Drop the seeds on top of the compost with space between them. Sprinkle a little more compost on top. Add a label and water. Place in a warm and sunny place.

step 2

The little seedlings don't like to be overcrowded. Gently pick some out so there is about 3cm (1in) between each one.

step 3

Water often but don't add feed to the water. Radishes and onions are not in the compost for very long so don't have time to get hungry.

step 4

Pull up the radishes and the onions when they are 3cm (1in) long. Sow a pot of radishes and onions every three weeks. You can grow them until the autumn.

Plant in the spring!

Tumbling tomatoes

Homegrown tomatoes taste great! Pick them from the plant and pop them in your mouth. Grow 'tumbler' tomatoes. Their little fruits tumble down your pot and do not need support.

Things you need

- Seeds ('tumbler' variety)
- Tray • Compost • Small and big pots • Bits of broken pot • Plant food
- Watering can • Labels

Plant in the spring!

step 1

In spring, place some compost in a pot. Press some seeds into the compost and water.

step 2

Put broken bits of pot into a big pot. Fill the pot with compost. When your seeds have grown into seedlings, dig a hole in the compost and plant one seedling.

step 3

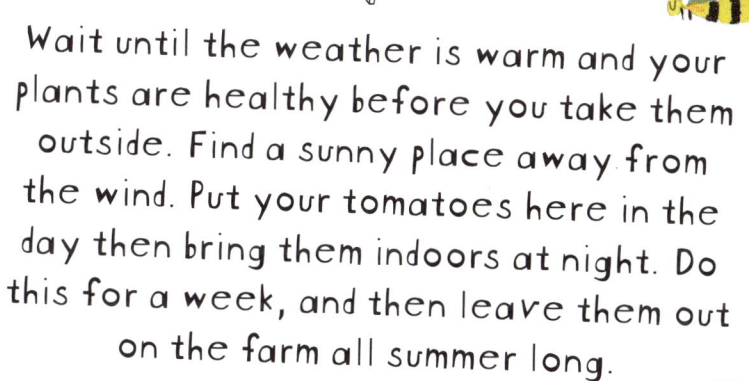

Wait until the weather is warm and your plants are healthy before you take them outside. Find a sunny place away from the wind. Put your tomatoes here in the day then bring them indoors at night. Do this for a week, and then leave them out on the farm all summer long.

growing tip

Once you see the tomatoes appear, add plant feed to their water once a week.

Tummy treats

Turn your tomatoes into a pasta sauce. Pick a big bowl of tomatoes and rinse under running water. Put them in a shallow oven tray and add chopped onions or garlic, olive oil, salt and pepper and some herbs that you like. Ask a grown-up to roast them in a hot oven for half an hour. Yum!

Crunchy courgette and summer squash

These come in lots of different shapes and colours, and if you give them plenty of water and sunshine they will grow and grow.

Things you need

- Seeds • Small and big pots
- Broken bits of pot
- Compost
- Plant food
- Watering can • Labels

Plant in the spring!

step 1

In spring put broken bits of pot into little pots. Fill with compost and push one seed into the centre of each pot. Water and keep indoors.

step 2

When it's warm outside and your plants have three or four 'true' leaves (not the little ones that first appear) plant outside in big pots in a sunny spot. Use the largest pots you have.

step 3

Water a lot and, when the first flowers appear, add liquid feed to the water once a week.

step 4

The fruits grow out of the big yellow flowers. Pick when they are about 10cm (4in) long.

Tummy treats

Ask a grown-up to chop lots of types of courgette and squash into chunks and place on a skewer to barbecue.

Fabulous Fruit

Down on Flowerpot Farm, the buzzing bees love visiting the fruit garden and pollinating the plants and fruit trees. As the plants grow, little flowers appear. These are called blossom and, after the bees have visited, the blossom turns into little fruits.

It's summer!

Sunshine makes the fruits grow bigger and bigger ... until they are sweet enough to eat.

Did you know that over half the food we eat relies on bees pollinating plants?

Scrummy strawberries

Start growing strawberries in spring and by summer you'll be enjoying lots of these scrummy little fruits.

Things you need

- Small strawberry plants
- 3 different-sized pots
- Broken bits of pot
- Watering can
- Plant food
- Compost

Plant in the spring!

step 1

Put some broken bits of pot in the bottom of each flowerpot.

Fill the pots up with compost and stack them with the biggest pot on the bottom and the smallest on top.

step 2

Dig several little holes around the edges of the two largest pots and in the top of the smallest one. Put your strawberry plants in the holes.

step 3

Water your strawberries every day. Once a week add some feed to the water.

step 4

Choose a sunny spot to grow your strawberries, out of the wind.

step 5

When the fruit has turned red all over pull it gently away from the stalk. It's ready to eat. Yum!

Flag up your strawberries!

Draw a large triangle on a piece of fabric. Cut it out. Fold in half and decorate on both sides. Glue a lollipop stick along the fold. Glue the two halves together and plant in the pot.

my strawberries

Amazing apples

Special little apple trees called 'step over apple trees' are perfect for growing in very big pots. They grow all year round.

Things you need

- 'Step over apple tree'
- Very big pot
- Broken bits of pot
- Compost
- Plant food
- Watering can
- Label

Plant in the autumn!

step 1

Choose the biggest flowerpot you can find. It should be 45cm (18in) or bigger. Find a sunny place out of the wind. Put in lots of broken bits of pot and half fill with compost.

step 2

With grown-up help, pull the apple tree out of the pot it came in and put in the middle of your big pot.

growing tip

Plant your apple tree in November. Keep it well watered, even in winter, and free from weeds. When the first flowers appear feed it every week until the apples are ripe.

step 3

Fill up the pot with compost and give it a good watering.

Tummy treats

Dried apple rings make a delicious snack. Ask a grown-up to help you take out the core of an apple and slice it into rings. Soak them in a bowl of cold water with lots of lemon juice. Drain and thread onto a piece of string. Peg up the string high in a warm, dry and airy room. After a few days they will be ready to eat. Yummy!

Beautiful blueberries

Blueberries have white flowers that turn into deep-blue fruits. In autumn the leaves turn orange then fall off. Don't worry! They'll grow back again next spring.

Blueberries grow all year round. If you have room on your farm plant two different varieties. You'll have more fruits.

Things you need

- Blueberry bush
- Very big pot
- Broken bits of pot
- Ericaceous compost
- Plant food
- Watering can
- Label

Plant in the autumn!

step 1

Choose the biggest flowerpot you can find. It should be 45cm (18in) or bigger. Put it in a sunny spot out of the wind. Put broken bits of pot in and half fill with compost.

growing tip

Collect rainwater in buckets and use it to water your blueberries. They love it!

step 2

Pull the blueberry bush out of the pot it came in and put in the middle of your big pot. Fill it up with compost and water it well.

Tummy treats

Add blueberries to your breakfast cereal, or eat with ice cream or pancakes. If you have lots, ask a grown-up to freeze them.

step 3

When the flowers appear feed your blueberry bush every week. When the fruits turn deep blue they are ripe. You can pick and eat them. Yummy!

Bitter lemons

A lemon tree will grow on your fruity farm all year but, if the winter is cold, bring it indoors in autumn. Lemon trees hate frost and snow!

Things you need

- Lemon tree • Big pot
- Broken bits of pot
- Ericaceous compost • Plant food
- Watering can • Label

Plant in the spring!

step 1

Put lots of broken bits of pot in a big pot and half fill with compost.

step 2

Pull the lemon tree out of the pot it came in and put it in the middle of your big pot. Fill it up with compost and give it lots of water.

step 3
Feed it once a week and water it all through the year.

Grow a fruit tree
Plant a pip from a lemon, orange or apple 3cm (1in) deep in a little pot of compost. Water, label and wait to see if it comes up!

Tummy treats
Use your lemons to make lemonade. Put one cup of water and one cup of sugar in a heavy saucepan. With grown-up help, heat and stir until all the sugar melts and you have a thick syrup. Squeeze juice out of six lemons. Put the juice in a jug with the syrup. Add three cups of cold water. Stir and put in the fridge for half an hour.

Flowerpot Farm Friends

Everything in the world is here for a reason: you, me, birds, worms, butterflies and bees. We are all important! Be kind to these creatures and they will become your friends and helpmates on Flowerpot Farm. Share your flowers, fruit and vegetables with bees and ladybirds and see how well your garden grows!

Rain is good!

Sunshine is nice but farmers like the rain too! Remember that water is just as important as sunshine for bumper crops, so never waste it.

Ladybirds and hoverflies are good garden guests but need to eat bad garden pests for their dinner. Don't use nasty sprays on pests or the good guys will go hungry!

Meet the Pollinators

anther

pistil

Sit quietly among your flowerpots and watch how bees and butterflies busily swoop from flower to flower. They are doing a very important job—making seeds to create next year's plants. This is called pollination, and the insects that do it are called pollinators.

How pollination happens

A hungry pollinator visits a flower to drink the nectar on the plant's pistil. While they drink this delicious sweet liquid their wriggling bodies and flapping wings get covered in yellow dust. This is pollen and it comes from the part of the plant called the anther.

Making a seed

When a pollinator flies away to visit another flower, tiny spots of pollen are rubbed off and fall onto that flower's pistil. Inside the pistil, eggs are waiting for the pollen. The pollen turns the eggs into seeds — the precious things we need to grow new plants.

Wind and weather

Not all plants are pollinated by insects. Some, like sweetcorn and grasses, have their pollen blown by the wind until it finds another plant. Bees don't like the cold and wet and often stay at home on rainy days.

The best flowers for pollinators

Just like you, bees have their favourite colours too!

Bees love blue, purple, violet, white and yellow.

Insects come in all sizes so grow small flowers as well as big ones on your Flowerpot Farm.

Meet the Garden Guests

bees

Bees, butterflies, dragonflies, ladybirds, beetles, toads and frogs are all garden good guys. They keep your plants happy and healthy. In order to welcome good garden guests to your farm, plant lots of flowers with different shapes and colours.

butterflies

hoverflies

Hoverflies love to feast on garden pests. They are very pretty and have stripes like a bee.

ladybirds

Ladybirds eat lots and lots of aphids. Aphids love to eat juicy plants.

bats

Bats are night-time garden good guys. They love to eat lots of insect pests. Bats like big, white or pale-coloured flowers with a strong smell as they are easier to find in the dark!

ground beetles

Ground beetles hunt at night, too. They eat up lots of plant pests. Take a torch into the garden after dark and see if you can spot them. Watch you don't stand on any though!

frogs and toads

You are very lucky if you have frogs and toads in your garden. They eat slugs and keep your lettuces safe.

Drinks for your friends

Make sure that the garden good guys have lots to drink when they visit your farm. Fill a tray with water and add some pebbles to stop the smaller creatures falling in. Put the tray in a quiet spot in the shade. Don't forget to keep it filled up with water.

Wriggling worms

Worms are very important. They wriggle through soil and compost letting in air. They eat rotting plants, turning it into rich compost that feeds the earth. Dig carefully in the soil to find a few earthworms. Use these to start your very own worm home, called a wormery.

Things you need

- A large clean glass jar or fish tank with a lid with holes
- Compost • Sand • Earthworms
- Vegetable peelings, tea bags, old leaves, old fruit
- Black paper
- Newspaper

step 1
Put 1cm (½in) of sand at the bottom of the jar or tank.

step 2
Add a 5cm (2in) layer of compost and a 1cm (½in) layer of sand.

step 3
Add layers until there is a space of 5cm (2in) at the top. Put in your worms. Watch how they wriggle down into the soil.

step 4

Add the vegetable peelings, tea bags, old leaves and old fruit. Cover with a damp sheet of newspaper.

step 5

Put on the lid. Make sure it has holes in it so the worms can breathe.

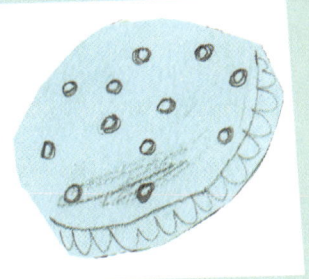

step 6

Wrap black paper around the jar or tank and place in a cool, dark cupboard. After two weeks remove the paper and see what has happened!

Your wormery

Top up your wormery every two weeks with vegetable waste and damp newspaper. Worms don't like daylight, so don't let them out of the dark for too long. When the worms have turned all the vegetable waste into lovely rich compost, empty it out and use in your pots.

Meet the Garden Pests

Lots of creatures and insects visit your farm but not all are welcome! Here are some tips to help you keep keep your plants safe.

slug

snails

Slugs and snails eat almost any plant. They feed at night. In the morning you can see their silvery trails. By day they hide in dark and damp places such as under big leaves.

Slugs and snails don't like to feel crunchy things. Crush up the shells from a boiled egg and put them on top of the compost in your pots.

aphids

flower buds

Aphids are little pests that cause big damage. They just eat and eat! They gather in groups on flower buds, the tips of stems and underneath leaves. They are white, green, black, brown and even yellow. Tie Christmas tinsel around your pots to scare them off!

Winter on the Farm

top

bottom **bulb**

There's not much to do on the farm when it's cold and wet outside. A good job for indoors is planting flowering bulbs. Crocuses, daffodils, hyacinths and tulips can all be planted in autumn.

Don't tidy away fallen leaves, old grass or bits and bobs around your pots. All kinds of creatures like to hide away and sleep in these dark and cosy places!

Planting indoor bulbs

Half fill a pot with compost. Put in the bulbs close together, but not touching. Make sure you plant your bulbs the right way up! Fill the pot with compost. Water and put it in a cold, dark place. Water twice a week. After **10** weeks bring the pot into a warm, light room. Watch the shoots appear and then the flowers.

beetles

Make your own bird food

Ask a grown-up to melt some fat (lard or suet) in a pan and stir in a dry mix of kitchen scraps such as breadcrumbs, cheese, oats, currants and sunflower seeds. Use twice as much dry mix as fat. Stir until thick and sticky. Ask a grown-up to help you make a hole in the bottom of a yoghurt pot and pull a piece of string through it. Pour in the fat mix. Leave in the refrigerator overnight to set. Cut away the yoghurt pot and use the string to tie the bird food to a tree.

Water tray

Even in winter keep a shallow tray full of drinking water on the farm for birds, animals and insects.

Index

aphids 54, 59
apples 44-45
bats 55
bees 16, 29, 41, 52, 53
beetles 55
bird food 61
blueberries 46-47
blossom 41
bulbs 60
butterflies 16, 29, 52, 54
chives 24-25
compost 9
courgettes 38-39
feeding plants 9
flowers 16-27
frogs 55
fruit 40-49
hoverflies 51, 54
labels 14-15
ladybirds 51, 54
lemons 48-49
lemonade 49
lettuces 32-33
marigolds 18-19
nasturtiums 22-23

onions 34–35
plant pots 8, 15
pollinators 52–53
potatoes 30–31
radishes 34–35
seedlings 11, 12–13
seeds 9, 10–11
slugs 55, 58, 59t
snails 58, 59
sowing 10–11
squashes 38–39
strawberries 42–43
sunflowers 26–27
sweet peas 20–21
toads 55
tomatoes 36–37
tools 9
vegetables 28–39
wormery 56–57

Goodbye from Flowerpot Farm

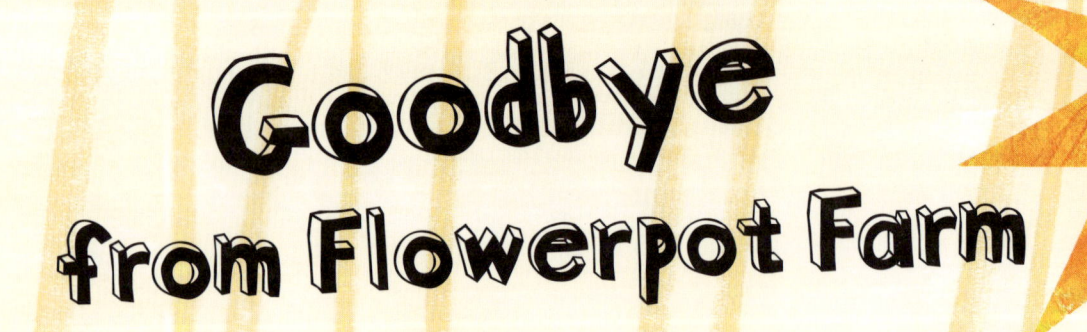

Why not...

Make a big wall chart with a box for each month of the year. Plan what seeds to sow when. Decorate it with pictures of birds, butterflies and bees!

Keep a picture diary or scrapbook to show how your farm changes over the months. Take photos, draw pictures, paste in old seed packets, recipes, pictures of what you want to grow next year, or whatever takes your fancy!

Start a gardening club with your friends. Share tools, swap seeds, have a competition to see who can grow the fattest courgette or tallest sunflower!